MY SON WENT TO JAIL FOR TAKING A BATH

A "MUST READ" For Every Parent and Their Teenager

LORRAINE HOLMES MILTON

AuthorHouse™ LLC
1663 Liberty Drive
Bloomington, IN 47403
www.authorhouse.com
Phone: 1-800-839-8640

Published by AuthorHouse 11/27/2013

ISBN: 978-1-4918-1318-8 (sc)
          978-1-4918-1319-5 (e)

Library of Congress Control Number: 2013916067

I dedicate this poem to my Beloved Mother,
Sylvia Mae (Glover) Solomon.

Lorraine Holmes Milton, Lieutenant, USNR, MSC

Lorraine Holmes, US Air Force (Enlisted) - 1976

I Am My Mama's Child

I am my Mama's Child

I am my Mama's Child

Thank you, Thank you, Thank You

I am my Mama's Child

If I did something to hurt you

I am so sorry

You were always there for me

I want you to be proud of me

I want to Thank you, Thank you, Thank you I am my Mama's Child

I am my Mama's Child

I am my Mama's Child

You gave me courage and strength

You're the greatest Mama in the World.

Mama, Mama, I love you

Mama, Mama, I love you

Mama, I Love You.

Lieutenant Lorraine Holmes

Bride and Groom, Patrina and Allister's
Wedding, December 29, 2012

Allister, Lorraine (Mom) and Eric -Photo taken shortly after
Allister's release from prison TDCJ, July 2011

Do you know that you can be shot down like a dog that stole something just because you are playing with a plastic toy weapon (gun)?

<u>Yes, you can!</u>

It depends on the time, place, circumstances, etc. When my son was a teenager, eighteen years old, he became friends with the wrong crowd. It was late at night (near midnight), the police was knocking loudly at the door because a warrant was issued for my son who had taken a bath. I all started around twenty (20) years ago when my eldest son, Allister Leon, was eighteen years old. Allister had been voted the President of the Student Council at a private and prestigious School in San Antonio, Texas, Holy Cross Catholic School. It was a great school academically, socially, and sportsmanship. Allister had many friends and was very popular.

Excerpt from **Pinnacle: Poems That Will Inspire You**
This is my second published book.

PRISONERS

Prisoners are people like you and me

They made a mistake and did something wrong

They need love, caring and to belong

The prisoners need rehabilitation

not manipulation

Education and counseling

May be the key

It should be mandatory

Before they can be set free

Teach them skills

To learn how to pay bills

So they won't steal

Take away their sob

So they won't rob

Send them mail

While they sit in their cell

Send them a book

To deter them from being a crook

I plead to this nation

Give the prisoners an education

Pray for them to make a positive change

and reach their full potential

It will be beneficial

<u>POTENTIAL</u>

Reaching your full potential should be strived

It is possible if you try

Articulate, investigate, facilitate

Negotiate, mitigate and do whatever

It takes

Apply yourself until there isn't much left

Determination under the whole person concept

Is a good start

Vertical achievement is your right

Take advantage with all your might

I served twenty-one (21) years in the military. Allister was five years old when he arrived at Dover Air Force Base, Delaware in 1975 after my mom, his grandmother (second mom), suddenly became ill and passed away in January 1975. Allister was four (4) years old and devastated. I was so saddened and hurt, hollow, and hopeless to have lost my dear beloved mother. My friend, Mary Stockton (later married to Gerome Thompson) accompanied me to Detroit to attend my mother's funeral. I am forever grateful for the compassion Mary had shown during my time of grief and sorrow.

<u>MOTHERS</u>

Mothers cherish their children

and protect them with their

inner strength

Mothers stay up all night

To care for their sick child

When they need to sleep a while.

Mothers give their children their last

Sometimes slow and many times fast

Mothers know when their child

Needs a motivational lift

It is the mother's spiritual gift

Mothers have fine intuition

Their thoughts usually

Come to fruition

A mother's love and devotion

To her child is not

Like any other

Allister went to Kindergarten in 1975 while I was stationed at Dover Air Force, Delaware. He had many activities like other dependent children - Alister flourished. Thank you, Roxanne Ward Graves for assisting Allister and me while I performed military duties.

I was a single parent until Allister was six (6) years old (more on that later).
In 1976, I married Gerald Francis Holmes, an Air Force Staff Sergeant. He and Allister gelled well together. We received military orders in 1981 to Myrtle Beach Air Force, South Carolina. Allister was eleven (11) years old.

Allister is very smart and received very good grades. His behavior in school was in question at various times mentioned the teachers. One thing worth noting is that Allister is very organized –both externally and internally. He keeps good, detailed records of mail, bills, schedules, and everything and he can remember situations when he was two (2) years old. I can barely remember two (2) weeks ago.

In 1978, Allister's baby brother, Eric Terrill, was born. Allister was so happy to have a brother – the whole family was happy-I was ectstatic. Eric attended private school, too; Saint Mary's Hall is a very rich academically, financially, historically, and all around a wealthy school. Eric grew up and graduated from Morehouse College, Atlanta, Georgia. Let's get back to Allister taking a bath and going to jail. In 1983, we received military orders to Lackland Air Force Base, San Antonio, Texas. Gerald was selected to become one of the "Cream of the Crop" positions – Technical Instructor (TI), a much sought after military position training Basic Airmen. Allister continued to progress well in school, football, track and field, etc. I truly believe that if we were stationery and Allister had obtained a good coach, he would have been an Olympian. Sometimes I think that military families should get compensation due to the missed opportunities due to their frequent moves.

In 1978, I started going to college while at Dover and attended school off and mostly on until December 1996- eighteen years of higher education. I love learning. I have four college degrees, including two (2) Master's Degrees.

Some people say that his father and I was so busy with our military career and attending school that we lost track of our son. **Response:** The military is a 24/7 job. We were placed on-call many weekends and weekdays and it was mandatory. We did not have a choice as to whether to call in sick, not go to work or whatever. There are many Presidents/CEOs, both men and women, who attended college and at the same time raised a family. This was one of the primary reasons they attended college was to make a better living for their families.

We, in the military, gave up our rights to protect your rights!

***I did not know that my mom was going to suddenly take ill.

***I did not know that Allister was spending time with the wrong crowd while we were at work.

***Allister was taught to behave, go to school, be polite, use his manners, just like most children from respectable families.

***The military promotes individuals who strives for upward mobility, such as, higher education.

***I did not know that when I walked out the front door to go to work, he walked out the back door to be with his friends.

***No, I did not put my career over my son's well being. He was a teenager – like most teenagers "know everything and don't know anything."

***Allister seemed to be doing just fine when we were home together as a family.

We were clueless to Allister's illegal activities!

Some teenagers can surely hide symptoms from their parents. I am one person that has a keen intuition – it isn't easy to skip pass me (figuratively). Sometimes I look back and say, how did I miss the signs of Allister getting into trouble.

Questions to All Parents:

How can you blame yourself when one child goes wrong and the other child goes right? Each person has an opportunity, on a daily basis, to make prudent choices.

I was commissioned in the U.S. Navy in 1985 and stationed in Camp Lejeune, North Carolina in 1986 for a year. Gerald did not accompany me. We were divorced in 1987. Allister was sixteen. I bought him a Mazda 626, Red, car for his sixteeth birthday. Allister would drive back and forth through the Base Gate just so the guards would salute him (the car had an Officer's Blue Sticker). It really concerned me when I found out (twenty years later). The Mazda was crashed in North Carolina – Allister was fine. In 1987, we moved back to San Antonio, Texas and bought a newly built house. My sister Pearlene resided with us. One day, shortly after moving back to San Antonio, Allister was caught in the garage with several teenagers. Pearlene confronted him. I was at work on the base. I did not allow any socializing, loitering, or anything of such to be going on at the house without me being present. The following year, his cousin (my niece) Sylvia (in Foster Care in Detroit), moved with us – she was thirteen (13) years old and Allister was seventeen. They were very close and chummy buddies. Soon they started mischievous behavior together. They would sneak out the window at night while I was asleep. It was a rollercoaster year – one thing or another was always happening. I sought counseling for Allister – Sylvia refused to talk with the therapist. Allister didn't want to attend school anymore and took the General Equivalent Diploma (GED) and passed. Allister is very smart and sometimes astute. His decision to let his social buddies influence him negatively led him to pay a tall price.

<u>BUDDIES</u>

The buddy I know

He and I went toe to toe

We continue to be friends

throughout thick and thin

Me and my buddy

Have unspoken rules

Chill out, watch games,

Be cool, and stay in school

My buddy cheered me up

When I was in a rut

Buddies always have your back

Their friendship and bond

Is second to none.

Both children attended private, religious schools and yet Allister found a way to go astray. Allister is a real good son and I adore him. He is witty, well-spoken, charming, meticulous, intelligent, courageous, athletic, model dresser, and tenacious.

When Allister was eighteen years old he decided to go to a Hardware Store with his friends to rob the store – Allister had a plastic toy weapon (gun). His sentence was over fifteen years- he served twenty years in Texas Department of Corrections.

<u>A Plastic Toy Weapon (gun).</u>

PARENTS:

Please know this: If your child is playing with a toy gun at the wrong place and uses it in the wrong fashion, he could be shot and killed or arrested. Allister was arrested.

I had just arrived in Yokosuka, Japan to serve a three (3) year tour of duty when I received the dreaded call –Allister was arrested for using a plastic toy gun in a robbery.

According to the Prosecutors, the fright of the "toy gun" was just as real as a "real gun."

Allister would have traveled to Japan with the family; the military disapproved his travel request due to the previous trouble- I was very upset. I didn't have a choice- I had to go.

PARENTS:

Please discuss the importance of honesty with your children. I discussed all "the talks" with Allister. They say a person has to go to "The School of Hard Knocks" or "They Made their bed – Let them lie in it." I believe that you can remake your bed and become an upstanding citizen in society.

I know by now you are wandering, why did she name the book, **"My Son Went To Jail For Taking A Bath"** because it is true.

Once or twice he was paroled and had to wear a Tether monitor (ankle bracelet) for approximately sixty (60) days. He went back to prison for violation of parole (VOP). I had paid thousands of dollars to numerous attorneys to represent Allister while I was stationed Overseas and when I returned home. In 2011, Allister was up for parole again, his attorney,

Tammy Peden of Houston, Texas, a great attorney, represented him to the maximum. Allister was released July 2011. We were elated. Allister placed many resumes online to no avail. The majority of companies have a standing policy that they will not hire Felons for a specified timeframe – Allister did not meet the guidelines. Allister found a job at the Car Wash – he was employed. He was adamant concerning finding immediate employment. His friend could not get his monitor taken off because he did not have a steady job. Allister started taking college classes and things were looking up. He purchased a Mercedes Benz. You may say "how can a person afford a Mercedes working at a Car Wash." In Texas, Car Washes are BIG BUSINESS. The average car wash is approximately $20. In Greater Detroit, Michigan, the average car wash is approximately $4 - $5 and that is a big difference.

Yes, the future was looking very bright.

One day Allister came home very tired, feet hurting, back breaking and walked slowly in the door. I said, Allister you should take a hot Jacuzzi bath with the jets – it will relax your muscles and make you feel better. Allister was working very diligently and was very tired from working at the Car Wash. Now, he works for a Global Company. Allister decided to take the Jacuzzi bath and stayed in the bathtub about thirty (30) minutes – it was around 5 o'clock because like I mentioned earlier Allister is very keenly aware of everything. He went to visit his Parole Officer (PO) the next day on a regularly scheduled visit; he was told that a WARRANT was issued for his ARREST. The PO told him that a report said the monitor was not activated from approximately 5 o'clock until 5:30 p.m. the previous day. Allister said, I was taking a bath in the Jacuzzi bath tub. The PO understood and told him to go on to school and go home afterwards and stay home.

Allister's previous PO visited our home before Allister's release to explain the rules.

These are some of the rules:

1. A Landline telephone must be active at all times.

2. Allister will wear a Tether Monitor for a minimum of one year. If all the guidelines are followed then the monitor will be removed. Allister walked a chalk line and the Tether Monitor was removed exactly one year.

3. Allister must stay at home (indoors) at all times when not working. He could not go on the porch, patio, back yard , mail box, no where unless it was on the weekly schedule.

4. All work and appointments must be documented on the schedule.

5. Do not schedule work between midnight and seven – it must have a special approval.

6. If he wanted to go to Church – it must be on the schedule.

7. Allister must attend Twelve Step Program.

8. Do not submerge monitor under water. (They did not tell Allister or either they forgot to tell him or Allister forgot that they told him. It must be the former. Allister remembers keenly.)

9. Allister was approved to attend Aspire To Win Program.

Attorney Peden recommended this awesome program for prisoners who has served, at least, ten (10) consecutive years incarceration. The program was founded by Rosey Ruiz – a book needs to be written exclusively about this program because it has assisted so many people and reduced the recitivism rate. The essence of the program is comraderie, compassion, motivation, self-esteem, education, counseling, support system and so much more. I am truly grateful for Attorney Peden for recommending Aspire To Win and to the Founder, Rosey Ruiz for accepting and embracing my wonderful son, Allister. Aspire To Win has assisted Allister tremendously- even though he has graduated he attends meetngs when his work schedule permits. Allister is aspiring to WIN and I'm so proud of him. Allister will speak at different high schools to motivate and encourage students to stay in school and not let the wrong people influence them. Everyone makes mistakes – the important point is to learn from them. Becoming a Life Coach and Motivational Speaker is in his horizon. He has a lot to say.

<u>**WINNING**</u>

Winning is the goal

No matter if it takes a toll

Winning is the name of the game

Whether you are tame or have fame

Winning is something you strive for

Then go after more

Winning is doing your best

And passing every test

Winning is showing your strength

And inner core

At the same time

Continuing to soar

Win in all your endeavors

Then you'll reach a higher level

Win until you're tired

You'll get hired

Put winning in perspective

and be selective.

<u>WISDOM</u>

Knowledge is an important tool

Let us listen while in school

When you know what you supposed to know

It is a good sense of awareness

Even if you have to say so

Learning will always be in style

The wise seems to fair better

The love of learning is a wise habit

The knowledge in return

Motivates you to learn

It's so important to be in the know

It can be for World Peace and not for show

Study diligently and self-educate

For your benefit and the world's sake

now that you are vey important

Your efforts will be contingent

On a futuristic better place.

The police officers (around 4) knocked loudly at the door – **BAM-BAM-BAM** on the door as if to knock the door down. It was very late at night. Allister had said earlier, I'm not going to answer the door. I said, you should answer the door. Allister said, I didn't do anything wrong.

I said, I know – just let them straighten it out. They will know that you **ONLY took a bath.** The police went to the back door and **BAM-BAM-BAM. It** seemed **that the door was going to shatter because half of the back door is glass.**

Allister figured it out that they were not leaving without him so he walked slowly downstairs and opened the door.

It broke my heart to see that all this commotion was activated due to a **BATH!**

Allister answered the front door. I started walking towards the door and the police **flashed a Gigantic Spotlight in my face.** I**I stopped COLD! Frozen!**

I slowly turned around and walked towards the
Family Room.

Allister was ARRESTED for TAKING A BATH!

I was so sad. I went to the vestibule and told Allister "It will be okay. We will pray" or something to that affect - It seems like a blurr.

Like Oprah says, What do you know for sure?

1. I know that it is unfair to have a system that can't distinguish a bathtub.

2. It is unjust to be arrested for taking a bath.

3. It is unfair to serve twenty (20) years for playing Cops and Robbers. I am not minimizing what Allister did – he commited a crime. I am saying that the punishment does not fit the crime. There are murderers walking and driving the streets and have't served one day.

4. I know **I AM VERY ANGRY.**

5. I know that I feel responsible for Allister's arrest because I encouraged him to take a bath to soak and relax his aching bones.

6. I know the system is beyond broken and need to be revamped as soon as possible. It should be more uniform – a certain amount of time for every crime regardless of location (State), offender's color, creed, socio-economic level, gay, straight or whatever.

7. I know that no one is better than me and I am not better than no one.

8. I know you reap what you sow.

9. I know there is 1.2 million prisoners in the United States and the majority are Black.

10. I know that my family has been discriminated by the government for over twenty (20) years – It started when I was in the military stationed in Japan.

11. I know I wrote several Presidents of the United States and to no avail.

12. I know a lot of things, however, I know I need to finish this book now.

<u>PARENTS</u>:

I want you to know that if the Parole Officer gives you a briefing separately from your son or daughter , take many notes and ask for the information **in writing.**

This will give you the opportunity to refer back to your informational guidelines. **<u>This is a travesty of Justice!</u>**

Allister served four (4) days. This is 4 days to many. He is serving his time on parole and the time of many others.

Tell your children – **NEVER GET INTO TROUBLE, HENCEFORTH, YOU WON'T BE AFFECTED BY THE JUSTICE SYSTEM.**

<u>OPEN LETTER TO ALL TEENAGERS.</u>

Please listen to me, I'm on bended knee- I pray to God that you will hear: Please continue school and finish. Grow up to become a mature and prospering adult in society. Educate yourself and don't let others influence you to opt against your principles. Your parents have taught you well. Please **LISTEN TO YOUR PARENTS!**

Do not do anything that will land you in jail. When you are locked in the cells, your so-called friends will be busy doing their nails.

Some friends will be gaming (literally and figuratively) and some will be conniving They may not care, however, your parents will be there.
Don't get pregnant or get someone pregnant while you are a teenager. Whom can you count on day and night, now and forever- Your Parents-Good ole Mom and Dad. They will be there when you are sad. Respect them, listen to them, and make them proud of you – they deserve it and so do you.

<u>BEAUTIFUL</u>

Beautiful is the deep blue sea

And the Sun that shines on me.

Beautiful is the light blue sky

Below is the sea shells floating by

Beautiful is a full moon

Waiting for the sunset that shows

An ecstatic scene

Beautiful is a new baby

Wrapped in his mother's arms

Lying down peacefully

Life a beautiful charm

Beautiful noises fill the air

The birds are chirping in a pair

Beautiful is the snow and rain

They shower us as we go

About our plans

I am very proud of Allister. During all the twenty (20) years in the Texas Department of Criminal Justice he did not let the system "break him." Some prisoners had nervous breakdowns and flipped out under the stress and injustice. Many are medicated and in a different world.

I know the Criminal Justice system failed my son because I know there are thousands of people who has done outrageous crimes and only served one-quarter to half the time Allister served. Allister gives new meaning to **LIFE COACH because he has served LIFE!**

I think there may be a silver lining somewhere and somehow with this situation. It is difficult to understand. **<u>How can a Parolee be arrested for taking a bath when bank robbers are getting away with murder and the loot.</u>**

QUESTIONS.

1. Does the justice system provide justice?

2. What can you do to stay out of the justice system?

3. Should all children stop playing with toy weapons (guns) to prevent an arrest?

4. Why are some prisoners given lesser time for the same crime?

5. Is the Justice System broken?

6. Is it fair that parents have to serve the same sentence as their son/daughter?

7. What can we do, as parents, to encourage our children to plan on upward mobility and to be successful citizens, such as, finish school/Trade School, become an Entrepreneur, etc.

SINGLE PARENT.

Earlier, I mentioned that I would address this issue. Teenagers: It is not easy caring for your precious child while attending high school. I was fortunate in 1970 to attend a School for Unwed Mothers and graduated on time June 1970 at seventeen years old. I am very intelligent, however, evidently not smart enough not to avoid teen pregnancy. The hospital nurse said, I'll see you next year. I knew, I double knew that she would NOT see me (Many teenagers became pregnant every year) for many years on that Maternity floor. A teenager is still an adolescent until age twenty-one (21) years old according to the American Pediatric Association. How can a teenage child care for the demanding needs of a child? They do not have the maturity tools for parenting success. A matter of fact, I don't think it is fair to the child to have a teenage parent.

The child will be missing out on maturity, financial, social, and so much more if their parent is a teenager. You may think my mom will assist me with the baby. **NO! Do not put your child on your MOM. I did and my mom did not make it long caring for my son – only 6 months. Don't do it. Wait! It is not easy! You can have a baby when you are married after college.**

Statistics have shown that the majority of the prison population was born to teenage mothers.

Do you want to join the statistics – no, so wait, PLEASE!

Don't let anyone influence you to do anything that you do not want to do and you know is inappropriate. Listen to that inner voice that your parents and grandparents have been telling you. **Do what is right – not what you want to do right NOW. Your decision will last a lifetime.**

KEEP A GOOD ATITUDE.

Excerpt from **Perspectives: Poems That Will Touch Your Heart co-authored with my son, Eric Terrill Holmes.**

<u>GOOD ATTITUDE</u>

A good attitude is paramount

It'll determine your count

Your good attitude will show

That you already know

The rules of the game

Are not always the same

For some it is fun

And most it is already done

Your attitude will attest

That you are the best

You'll have a wonderful quest

As you sit at your mahogany desk.

You can have everything you want on a silver platter if you follow your goals and work diligently towards them.

<u>TIME</u>

Take time to:

Love

Hug

Enjoy

Celebrate

Smell

Taste

Listen

Exercise

Eat

Sleep

Be grateful

Be thankful

Be mellow

Converse

Pray

Read

Sing

Create

Dance

Date

Meditate

Apologize

Do Nothing

I received the idea of "Do nothing" from Eric. He works so diligently, just like Allister. Eric would say, I just want to "do nothing." Sometimes it pays to just be. If you do not take anything away from this book, please remember these points.

1. **Do not get pregnant or get someone pregnant.**

2. **Do not commit crimes.**

3. **Complete and finish school- go to college, Trade School or become an Entrepreneur.**

4. **Join the military – it builds character.**

5. **Remember your principles and do not let anyone influence you negatively.**

6. **Self-educate – read books, journals, newspapers, to improve yourself on a daily basis.**

7. **Engage in some of the activities in the "Time" poem.**

8. **Strive to be <u>healthy, wealthy and happy.</u>**

9. **Have a good attitude. Someone said, your Attitude determines your Altitude.**

10. **Strive to be the Best that you can be.**

11. **Invent, reinvent and make the world a better place.**

12. **Pray for World Peace.**

13. **Assist the homeless, disabled, elderly and sick – <u>Give Back Success.</u>**

14. **Count your blessings.**

15. **Honor Thy Mother and Thy Father, the Bible says.**

16. **Respect everyone – don't trust everyone.**

17. **When you go to sleep, can you say " I did something good for someone today."?**

18. **Drink plenty of waster and eat the proper nutrition.**

19. **Be prepared for disaster and assist your neighbors in disaster planning.**

20. **Exercise daily.**

21. **Get plenty of sleep.**

Allister's

Photo

Perspectives: Poems That Will Touch Your Heart
Pinnacle: Poems That Will Inspire You
Disaster Master Plan: Prepare or Despair - It's Your Choice.
Lorraine Holmes Milton, Author

Eric (top left), Allister, Antwan and
Kelven at Wedding

Allister and Dad (Donn Milton) at
Wedding December 29, 2012

Allister (Groom) and Patrina (Bride)

Annie Faye Newton , Teacher
(Mother of Kamilah S)

Eric and Kamilah Holmes on their Anniversary

Ellison Thierry Holmes and Elliott Townsend Holmes (Twins)
-Parents: Eric T. Holmes, Sr., and Kamilah S. Holmes

Patrina at daughter Shakora Johnson's High School Graduation, Greater Chicago,
May 2013. Father, Michael Ross, left and youngest son Deles Johnson, right

Allister and Patrina Holmes (Engagement)

Allister and Patrina's Wedding, December 29. 2012

Allister and Patrina's first day at new house as Mr. And. Mrs. Allister Leon Holmes

Best Man Antwan, and Groomsmen Kelvin pulling the Groom Allister (December 29, 2012)

Family Wedding Photo (December 29, 2012) Lorraine (Left, Groom's Mom), Allister (Groom), Patrina (Bride), Dora (Bride's Mom), Sylvia (Groom's 1st Cousin), Eric (Brother)

Groom Allister L. Holmes, December 29, 2012)

Mom (Lorraine Holmes Milton) and Groom (Allister Leon Holmes) Dancing at
Wedding (Allister and Patrina, December 29, 2012)

Allister L. Holmes and Dad (Gerald F. Holmes) at Wedding, December 29, 2012

Antwan, Allister L. Holmes (Groom), Kelvin, and Gerald F. Holmes (Allister's Dad)

Patrina (Hayes) Holmes

Donn James Milton and Lieutenant Lorraine Holmes at Navy Ball
(the main reason for us meeting each other)

Mary Ann Thompson. Best friend's since July 1975. Mary assisted with Allister and Eric's child rearing. She attended my mother's Funeral with me in February 1975.

Sharaya Cecelia Solomon hugging her brother, Devonte Doral Solomon Milton.

Mom (Lorraine Milton) and Son (Devonte Doral Solomon Milton).

Eric Terrill Holmes hugging Mother (Lorraine Holmes Milton)

Gerald Francis Holmes holding (grandsons) twins, Elliot Townsend Holmes and Ellison Thierry Holmes (Lorraine Holmes Milton is their paternal grandmother.)

LaRoyce Ray Nelson, US Army. (Ray is my sister Pearlene's youngest son).

Eric's Morehouse graduation Photo

Kamilah S. Holmes, Masters of Education Administration, Graduation at
University of Houston.

Lorraine and Donn Milton at Cavaliers Dinner Pensacola Florida 1997 Note The original does not show white on Donn's eyes, please crop it out

Patrina Holmes and Mom (Dora Washington) at Wedding, December 29, 2012

Lorraine, (Matriarch) Eric Sr.,, Donta, Donn (Patriarch), Sr., Kamilah, Allister (Back), Eric II,
Sharaya, Devonte (Front).

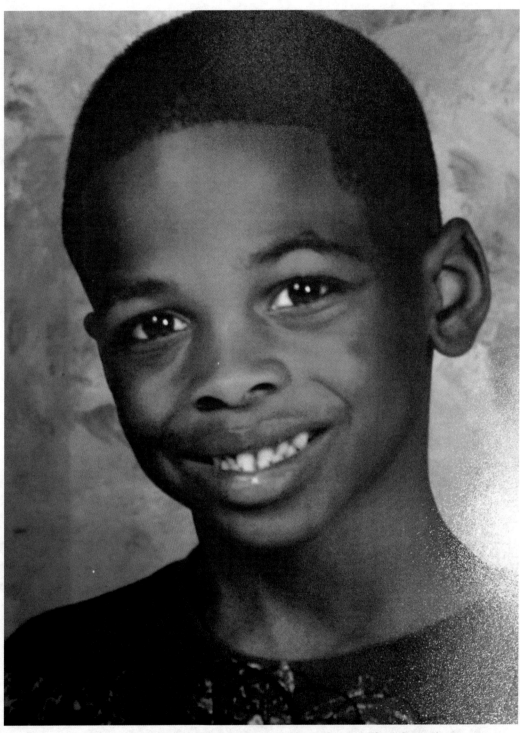

Devonte Doral Solomon Milton - Parents: Donn James Milton, Sr., and
Lorraine Holmes Milton.

DeJuan Pickens Hayes (Allister and Patrina's eldest son) attending Everest
College and on Dean's List with 4.0 average - #1

Rashida Graves, Roxanne Ward Graves (married to former US Air Force
Captain Harold Graves) and Ryan Graves (Roxanne and Lorraine-Best
Friends 1974 at Dover Air Force Base, Delaware)

Eric T Holmes, Kamilah S (Newton) Holmes, Eric T Holmes II and Elijah T Holmes

Grandchildren Elijah Tate Holmes, Ephraim Tobias Holmes and Eric Terrill Holmes II

Kamilah, Twins (Elliott and Ellison), Donn, Eric II, Elijah, Devonte, Ephraim, and Lorraine.

Allister Leon Holmes with youngest son, Deles Johnson. Allister loves his
Mercedes-Benz.

Lorraine Holmes attending Coastal Carolina College University of South Carolina 1982
Accepted to Scholarship Bootstrap Program from US Air Force

Allister and Eric

Eric is visiting Allister at TDCJ (prison), Sugar Land, Texas on April 21, 2002.
(Eric appears to be thinking, Why? It's been 12 years!)

Lorraine Holmes Milton, Dallas Love Airport, June 29,
2013, Power Networking Conference

Eric, Lorraine (My 3 Sons of 4), Allister and Devonte (Center)
(Allister and Patrina's Wedding, December 29, 2012.)

Eric Terrill Holmes, Sr., and Lorraine Holmes Milton (Mom) at
Allister and Patrina's Wedding, December 29, 2012

Sharaya Cecelia Solomon, great-niece, in Wayne County
Community College (WCCC) Jerseyn, currently a student a Wayne
State University

Printed in the United States
By Bookmasters